About the Author

Sabinah Adewole is a best seller and has enjoyed reading since childhood. She studied English and her poetry has been formed from her experiences on her journey through life, she has inspired a lot of readers across the globe. Journeys of Life Volume 2 is her second poetry book. Her first book can be found on Amazon and is available worldwide. She continues to use her poetry to inspire her audience.

Sabinah started writing poetry while sitting on a park bench in Gidea Park in May 2018. Her first poetry book Journeys of Life was published in Feb 2019, she has started to write children's poetry to inspire a younger audience. This book has captured poems written in Israel, Benidorm, Marbella, France and has been influenced from the various workshops she has been a part of. Sabinah has grown on the Poetry circuit, she has gone around various venues promoting her poetry. Her experiences show in her poetry.

Sabinah's poetry is informative for an everyday audience and would suit anyone from all crosses of life, her poetry is for everyone.

Some examples of her poems in this book are;

The Sea of Galilee; Watchman Nee; Bower House; Rejection; Gratitude; Believe; Swimming pool; What is fear? The Hospital and Diversity. Sabinah is passionate, creative, determined, enthusiastic with a positive mindset and this is captured in her poetry. She hopes that her poetry will have a lasting effect on all readers across the globe.

In her words

"If and when her words touch as many people, she is happy that She has fulfilled one of her goals in life"

About her writing

Sabinah's Poetry has been inspired by her faith. Several poems are centred around faith and she encourages the reader to develop his or her own faith. The message is a gentle one and not overly pushy. Her poems are written in free prose style bringing out the truth and beauty in everyday living. Some of her poems are classified as Epistolary; Allusion; How- to - poems; Object poems; Smell Poetry; Split or Cento poetry and Ekphrastic poems.

1

Reviews

"She gives each poem a particular spin, some bear a resemblance to sonnets others remind me of concrete poetry. The words themselves are used to create imagery or feeling."

"I feel as if the writer is dancing through life and inviting the reader to join in"

"Her poetry is optimistic, motivational and heart-warming" "The poems are about her travels and personal experiences"

"She is clearly a world traveller and poetically narrates her trips to various places "

"Her writing is described as very interesting and well acknowledged on the international circuit "

"Her poems have a hypnotic chanting quality, like the sacred psalms of the Old Testament."

The Beginning

Authors Acknowledgement

It has been a pleasure and privilege to write this book of my journeys and experience of an everyday life bringing out the truth and beauty in nature.

I have compiled a first volume of Journeys of Life which was published in February 2019 and I found this one of the most inspiring as I was not planning to do a Volume two straight away.

I have travelled to Israel, Benidorm, Marbella and France in compiling some of the poems in this volume. I have been in the company of my Husband on these vacations in the most beautiful locations.

I would like to thank my Husband Yinka who has stood by me , my older son Olly who provided me with the book cover from Tuscany while he was on vacation .

My son Olay and daughter Rebekah and the wider family.

I would like to thank especially Mary Walsh from my Poetry Group who studied the draft manuscript to make sure all relevant details were mentioned.

Others who have been immensely helpful are my Book page supporters who have engaged with my poems, the Growing poetry workshop I attend at the poetry library, the pen to print workshop, Spoken word London where I have gone to recite some of my poetry, and other circuits who have supported my journey and writing.

I am grateful for these opportunities and people who have personally supported my journey from the start through their encouragement and their reviews.

Index

1. About the Author
2. Acknowledgement
3. Index
4. Index
5. Index
6. The Sea of Galilee   101
7. The Fish Place Tamaris Restaurant   102
8. The Synagogue   103
9. On My Way to Jericho   104
10. The Tomb of the Prophets   105
11. The Pool of Bethesda   106
12. And So There Were Three   107
13. The Spiritual Man Watchman Nee   108
14. Bower House   109
15. Remembrance Sunday   110
16. Lanterns in the Barn   111
17. Diversity   112
18. The Train   113
19. The Black Bird on the Platform   114
20. Autumn   115
21. Waiting Area   116
22. The Hospital   117
23. Rejection   118
24. Christmas Times   119
25. Chocolate and Biscuits   120
26. Shows This Time of Year   121
27. Reflections   122
28. Patience   123
29. The Church   124
30. The Tango Tree   125
31. What is Fear?   126
32. It's a Time of Giving   127
33. The Friends Catch Up   128
34. The Youth of Tomorrow   129
35. Ladies Night Out   130
36. The Challenge of Writing   131

37. Gratitude 2018   132
38. The Local Theatre   133
39. My Day in Covent Garden   134
40. Snow Sleet   135
41. The Love Couple   136
42. The Happy Team   137
43. The Bridge on the A1   138
44. The Painting in the Mirror on the Wall   139
45. Benidorm   140
46. The Tour Guide   141
47. Valencia   142
48. The Fish Town Calpe   143
49. The Universal Painting caught my Attention   144
50. The Beach Walk - Mother and Baby   145
51. The Table Aquarium   146
52. The Beautiful Gates of Benidorm   147
53. Valentine   148
54. Silence   149
55. My Mother   150
56. The Librarian   151
57. The Swimming Pool   152
58. The Kayak   153
59. A Love of Libraries, Books andWonderful Words   154
60. The Tree House on the Foot Bridge   155
61. Women's Day   156
62. Believe   157
63. Life is a Journey   158
64. The Spice (Smell Speed Writing)   159
65. My Shadow   160
66. The Dome Rooftop   161
67. Anti-Hate   162
68. The Tulips in Reception   163
69. The Planters on the Dance Floor   164
70. The Beast in Cyberspace   165
71. Team Workshop   166

72. Sky is the Limit   167

73. Acrostic on Poetry   168

74. Stereoscopic Object Poetry   169

75. Seasons   170

76. Windmill   171

77. The Golf Course   172

78. The Black Power Bike   173

79. The Mystery Pair   174

80. Beauty Within Alien   175

81. Our Anniversary   176

82. My First Poetry Anniversary   177

83. The Beauty in the Lake   178

84. Rastafarian Dude on the Flight to Malaga   179

85. The Sports Car on the Drive   180

86. My Flowers Came with me to Marbella   181

87. Senegalese Boys on Levante Beach   182

88. The Party   183

89. Two Birds at the Breakfast Bar   184

90. The Tunnels   185

91. Smell was my Prompt   186

92. Two Ladies Communication   187

93. The Blue Motorised Tricycle   188

94. Pebbles   189

95. The Cat on the Drive   190

96. Electric Bikes in London   191

97. Our New Road   192

98. Town Centre   193

99. Beautiful Sunset   194

100. The Flower Girls   195

101. Couples   196

102. The Christmas Trees in the car park   197

103. The Amputee with a Stride   198

104. Centre Court   199

105. Pride in Wimbledon   200

The Sea of Galilee - 101

We went to see
We went to sea
It was a beautiful day
We had just been baptised in River Jordan
It was amazing
The rains came down after the baptism
We drove 20 minutes to board the boat
It was named Noah's ark
It was made from the finest wood
The boat sailed offshore
The sea was calm
We sang and danced
We prayed and took pictures
Our flag was raised on the boat
It was a good day to sail
It was an amazing presence of God
It was the love between us all
It felt good to be there
Where Jesus asked the fishermen to cast their nets
The Sea of Galilee
I challenge you to cast your nets and it shall not be
broken in Jesus name. Amen.

*I was inspired to write following our boat ride on the Sea
of Galilee*
Composed on the coach on 21/10/18

The Fish Place Tamaris Restaurant - 102

We arrived after the baptism
It was packed with tourists We
took our seats
We ordered our fish
There was a choice of fish or chicken
Majority went for fish
It was the special fish served in the restaurant It
came with rice or potato
We all had salad and Pitta bread
It was served with humus and some nice vegetables I
went to the bathroom
I walked past the main restaurant
There were loads of plates of fish and bones
The tourists had all enjoyed their fish
And left the bones to be cleared

Encourage young members to come on the pilgrimage
and enjoy the fish at the restaurant.
It was fresh and refreshing

Composed on the coach on 21/10/18
Inspired to write following eating Jesus fish in
Jerusalem.

The Synagogue 103

As I visit the home of Jesus
In Capernaum
I watch the pillars in the utmost state of
preservation
I sit and admire the statues in the blazing sun
I watch and listen to the gospel being preached
I sit and wonder what life could have been when
Jesus lived here Those 1000 years ago
I understand there were two levels above ground level
This is amazing I am inspired to write in the house
of Jesus
This would be my most inspirational poem
It's made from the finest stone
And I understand they were wealthy
people Jesus is wealthy
Matt 4:13
Made His home by
Capernaum
Success can be
geographical
Jesus had to move. He had to make an important
decision Change

*Was inspired to write in Capernaum the home of Jesus
on 22/10/18*
Composed in the synagogue in Israel.

On My Way to Jericho 104

As I sit on the Coach
We just left the home of Jesus
It's a two-hour drive
We drive past towns on the left Bethshean
Tee Eleseon
Jesus casts out evil spirits and transfers them to a herd of
pigs
They ran into the Sea of Galilee
We are privileged to see more than others that have come
before
We are on the eastern side of the Sea of Galilee
We have Jewish villages after 300 or 400 years after Jesus
We can see the hills on the left
We can see the Sea of Galilee on the right
It's such a relaxing drive with lots of scenery
The Romans built it
The city was on the mountain
With the zig zag road
There were ten cities
There was a lot to see
Eastern border of Israel on our way past River Jordan
On our way we stopped at the Mountain of Temptation
Then we arrived at the border of Jericho.
It is also known as the devil's town
It was the first city to be handed over to Palestine.
I challenge you to visit the oldest town in history

*I was inspired to write following my visit to the mountain
Composed on 23/10/2018 on the coach.*

*Was inspired to write in Capernaum the home of Jesus on
22/10/18
Composed in the synagogue in Israel*

The Tomb of the Prophets 105

Sitting down watching the dome in the centre of Israel
We sat and watched the tombs of the prophets
We walked down this steep walkway
We approached a beggar in the centre, bent over,
begging for alms
There are tourists and tourist walking by
This reminds me of "The Beggar" in the bible
When Jesus arrived, he said "Your faith has saved
you, rise up and walk."
We cannot judge anyone
We must do as Jesus did by recognising Difference
The dome is the mosque for the Muslims
The Muslims blocked the gate so as to discourage
Jesus from entering through that door
And decided to build the tombs of the prophets
The Tombs of the Prophets are huge and amazing
Lots of tombs to see
It reminds us of the cycle of life
Sunday Palm road Bethany
The largest Jewish cemetery in the world
This is the place that the Messiah will bring people to
life
The resurrection
The Tomb of the Prophets

Composed in the Tombs of the Prophets on 22/10/18
Inspired to write following a visit to Mount Olives.

The Pool of Bethesda 106

We arrived at the walls of Solomon
We walked through the
Jewish cemetery We arrived
at the Lions Gate
We walked past the birthplace of Virgin Mary
We arrived at Saint Anna Church which is famous for the
acoustics
We went down the stairs and took in the most amazing
works of excavation I met Cyndi from
Aberdeen in America
We arrived at Bethesda pool
We went down the stairs into the cave
We arrived at the pool we prayed, I felt a
transformation in my body My Knee was healed
I felt an overpowering presence once the
water touched me I had received my healing
I said thank you Jesus thank Jesus over a hundred times
stamping my feet I am blessed as this is where Jesus
healed the leper
I am healed

Inspired to write after use of the Bethesda pool.
Composed to write in the garden of Bethesda on 24/10/18.

And So, There Were Three 107

You have all heard of
The three wise men
The three Musketeers
Charlie's Angels the trio
This is all interesting that most good things come in three
Threesome
I was on my journey to Israel
Before I knew it there were three of us
She followed us everywhere we went
At the Mount of Transfiguration at Mount Olives
At the Western Wall
At the City of David on Mount Carmel
At the city of Jericho
On our way to Nazareth on the beach
At the Nativity church
At the tomb of Jesus, the Garden tomb
At the birthplace of Jesus
But the bad thing is the devil can tempt you
Even in the holiest of places
But the good thing as I did not give in
Never give up in the midst of temptation
Hold your ground no matter how hard they try
Wherever I turned the third person was there
In all my pictures But I never gave up
Just like the three wise men
They followed the star until they found Jesus
Never give up
Three is Challenging But you will overcome
Three is a journey that we all must take
Three is a number
I saw three trees at the home of Jesus in Capernaum
Three is a crowd At the foot of Jesus, she was exposed
God, came through for me

I was challenged to write this poem following my
experience in Israel
Inspired to write on the 4/11/18.

The Spiritual Man Watchman Nee 108

Witness Lee believed he was a witness
Need to give account of what they have seen
Gave up his job to serve the Lord
Watchman Nee
Believed to his glory
We're together in Shanghai in 1925
Met each other for the last time in 1950 in Hong Kong
Watchman sent witness Lee to Taiwan in 1949 to
continue the work
Arrested in March 1952 for the sake of the gospel
and sent to prison for 15 years until 1972 where he died.
A small note was found under his pillow
I die because of my belief in Christ this is the greatest
truth in the universe
I maintain my joy always rejoice and again I say rejoice
His wife had died six months prior
His body was cremated before his wife's sister got there
Watchman Nee remained faithful until the end
Praying in prison something was happening in the
spiritual realm Korea Malaysia China

Composed after my visit to Bower House.

Bower House 109

As we drove past Havering Atte Bower
We were on a mission to get more involved in our local community
We got a flyer through the post it was an open day
We had driven past a number of times
But never thought to delve into the local history
It took a flyer to invite us to this heavenly house
Which was now managed by Amanda Trust a Christian Charity
With a Bible college on site set up by a man with the name Witness Lee
What an interesting name that was because he believed he had to give witness to God's word through his works
We were met by a young man David who welcomed us and took us round to the marquee, We were welcomed with warm hands and smiles
We were invited to watch the video
It was wonderful as we did not know there was a Bible college situated in our community
10 minutes from my house
We were walking with Mary a Chinese student with her husband
This was a college with students from across the globe
They lived on site and some lived locally
It would seem we were being directed to something new
It would seem God brought us here for a reason
We were met by a lady Brenda who spoke about Bower House
It was a grade 1 listed mansion owned by John Bower and was the only listed building in Havering where I reside it had a 90-acre surrounding of green
But was now reduced to 9 acres it had a mural of paintings on the staircase
The staircase was made from the most beautiful oak wood imported from America. The painting was painted by a friend of John Bower who was known to have painted St Paul's Cathedral in London
The painting told stories of Greek mythology. As we sat I got a different perspective as less was said about Jesus and it appeared this was a movement of a Chinese involvement with Christ
Through the eyes of Watchman Nee and Witness Lee who were best friends and Watchman Nee sent Witness Lee to Taiwan to continue to spread the gospel Until it finally travelled to Europe and then America.
I challenge you to find encouragement in whatever your heart desires
God will lead you in the right direction Take a step of faith

Inspired to right following my visit to Bower house on 10/11/2018
Composed in my bedroom and finished in my living room on Remembrance Day on 11/11/2018.

Remembrance Sunday 110

I have often wondered about the meaning of Remembrance days
I know we sing the song God Save our Queen in the United
Kingdom
I am aware they wear the poppies
And there was a big display of poppies last year at Tower bridge
There was a big display this year of lighting 10,000 lanterns each
night until the build up to Remembrance Day
I have read so much on social media
And then realised what the poppies stand for
The red being the blood of the soldiers in the war
The black representing the mourning and the grief
The green leaves signifying growth and moving forward
In my house we always bought poppies at church but never knew
what they stood for I found out again on social media that
Remembrance Day was always celebrated on November 11th
each year. But now I understand that world war 1 stopped
on November 11th at the 11th hour and on the 11th day in the
11th month
This was interesting as so many people celebrate this around the
world
It has a global impact for all as a nation and in the world as a
whole to remember our fallen heroes
And for those that have lost someone through war
It brings back memories for us all
I pray our fallen heroes can continue to rest in peace as they
have made their nations and families proud.
We will continue to celebrate Remembrance Sunday as a
reminder for all the Veterans of war and a way of celebrating
them across the world.

*Inspired to write following a service at church today 11/11/2018
where we remembered our heroes.*

*Composed at home on 11/11/2018
Happy Remembrance Sunday across the globe
Inspired to write on Remembrance Sunday.*

Lanterns in the Barn 111

It was the most amazing first impression
There was music in the air
The air in the room was positive
The people were relaxed
It was the Barn Brasserie
It was wonderful
The beams stuck out from the ceiling
The decor was beautiful and inviting
You could not but notice the lanterns
They were shaped like a squash ball
Hanging from the ceiling
They were arranged in a line and were the centre piece in the barn
There were lights hanging in rectangular shaped coffin
They struck my attention
They had several colours which helped to light up the room
They were made from fabric
The lights shone through the colours
I have seen different lanterns in my lifetime
But these stood out and were captivating
I decided to write a poem about the lanterns in the barn
Next time you are in a restaurant
Check out your surroundings and see what items might interest you
And also, this reminded me to say hi
Always let your light shine through

Inspired to write following an invite to the barn
Composed on the train on the 15/11/18

Diversity 112

It was our inclusion week at work
All staff from different backgrounds
Arrived at the head office
Arrived wearing colourful outfits representing their culture
Arrived holding flags of many colours
Arrived explaining what flag was for what country
There was green white green
There was green white orange with a star
There was green black and a yellow strip across
There was green and red
There was blue white and yellow
I was impressed by the many colours
There was the rainbow flag
But they did not have one for Britain nor America
We took photos on the roof terrace
We took photos on the balcony
We held up signs saying what we stand for and what we
represent
Some were Muslims
Some were Christians
Some were Gay
Some were lesbian
I am so proud to work for such a diverse company
I am glad to have been part of an inclusive event
I challenge you to encourage diversity in your teams
I encourage you to promote inclusion always

Diversity I was inspired to write following an Inclusive
event on 20/11/18
Composed on the train

The Train 113

Has anyone experienced the feeling of arriving at the platform
and you jump on the train without checking
When you do this you are anxious to get to the next stop
As you are not sure if it's going in the right direction
Imagine if you were heading North and end up going south
This is why it is so important to plan ahead
So, we arrive at our destination with no anxiety
If we check the times
We would know when to arrive
We would know what train to get
We would know what time our train leaves
The issue is so many of us are hanging on to the train
Without realising if we are on the right train
We need to be ready
We need to be rest assured that we are on the right train
We all have a train to catch
As we are all heading some where
We all have a destination
We all know where we are heading to
We can all sit and enjoy our sandwich on the train
We can all sit and read a book and enjoy our time on the train
We can plug our phones
We can plug our headphones
We can sit and enjoy the scenery
We all must be ready to catch the next train
I was inspired to write after listening to the sermon in Church
today

Composed at home on 19/11/18

*My daughter had said to me to add attain on to the track on
my book cover yesterday*
*This is amazing that we speak of de-cluttering our houses so
we can be ready to catch the next train*
I challenge you to be ready to catch the next train
We should be ready to board anytime

The Black Bird on the Platform 114

As I sit at Romford station
I notice a black bird walking on the platform
I brought out my phone and started recording
The bird reminds me of myself as a child
The playful and carefree nature of a child
It reminds me of the bible where God says even
the birds of the air, I will take care of them talk-less
of us humans
We need to learn from the black bird
He was walking freely on the edge of the platform
He did not care who was watching
He was not bothered if he had makeup on or not
He was doing his own thing
God wants us to get up and do our own thing
today
Just like the bird took a risk and was walking the
walk
He wants us to talk the talk
I hope this poem has encouraged someone out
there today
I challenge you to take the step of faith trusting in
your own abilities

*Inspired to write seeing the black bird on the
Platform.*
Composed in the train on 23/11/18.

Autumn 115

It's that time of year
The leaves grace the pavements
The leaves are yellow and brown
They crunch as you walk on the grass
The leaves grace the floor
The leaves remind you it's Autumn
The leaves make you invite you to pick them up
The leaves need clearing out as they cause litter
The bin men have extra work to do
The leaves litter the ground
The leaves create an atmosphere
The leaves would do well in a video
The leaves would enhance an outdoor photo shoot
The children play with the leaves in the park
The dogs run around and play with the leaves in the park
The leaves fall in the lake
The leaves can be slippery when it's wet
The leaves can turn to ice in winter
The leaves can play hide and seek in the park
The children pick a handful of leaves in their hands
When is your favourite season in the year?
Mine is Autumn because of the colour of the leaves
Mine is Autumn as it represents a new beginning
All the trees shed their leaves and then it is Autumn
What's your favourite time of year?

Composed in my living room on 12/10/18
Inspired to write following an episode on autumn
leaves

Waiting Area 116

My daughter was unwell overnight
I called off from work
I was waiting in A and E
We had to wait for our turn
There were loads of people waiting
We were called for an assessment
They had red green black cards in order of priority of
need
We had to wait to be called
There were parents children, grandparents, women,
men, babies, toddlers all waiting in this one area
There were people with various issues all waiting to be
seen
We arrived at the right time
An argument broke out on the queue
He lost his temper with the nurse
The queue is all the way outside now
When we arrived, there were just two people before us
We are still waiting in the reception area
It's patience and focus that makes you last in such areas
It's nice to have company in waiting areas
It's nice to have a paper book your phone or magazine to
read in the waiting area
When next you're in a waiting area
Grab a book to read and focus on your self
It's a time and place to focus on your self
There so much that goes on in a waiting area

Inspired to write following a visit to A and E
Composed in Queens
waiting area on 29/11/18

The Hospital 117

Has anyone been to a hospital
It's the place that where you have the most people in their
uniforms proud of their qualifications and achievements
From the lower ranks to the highest ranks
The security staff
The health care assistants
The ambulance crew
The nurses
The ward managers
The doctors
The laboratory staff
The X-ray team
The surgeons
The consultants
Some wearing a stethoscope
Trying to save lives
I am not sure what we would do without them
I remember once when I was in hospital
They saved my life
We need to give thanks for having these people in our
hospitals
It's a place where so many people stay without realising
how fortunate we are
When next you are in a hospital for an appointment, blood
test, X-ray give thanks for these special people that have
been placed there as angels
The Hospital

*Inspired to write following a visit to the Queens hospital
on 23/11/18
Composed in A and E*

Rejection 118

Have you faced being rejected?
Have you been rejected before?
Have you lost friendships?
Have you felt people just do not understand who you are?
Do you feel God may be doing something in your life?
Do you feel you may be planted?
Do you feel you may be repositioning?
Do you feel that you can't take everyone with you to a higher level?
Do you feel that everyone cannot be happy for you?
Do you wonder why that is the case though?
Do you wonder that perhaps people might be dealing with their own issues?
When you meet anyone try and find out what they might be dealing with
Try and find out if you can be of assistance to help anyone
Rejection is not great but remember Jesus was rejected too in the bible
If you are a Child of God, he is preparing
you for greater things
Rejection makes you grow and
understand who you are

Composed in Queens hospital
Inspired to write following a reflection period on
28/11/18

Christmas times 119

The season is upon us
It comes around once in a year
We start our shopping early if we are organised
We put up the decorations in anticipation
We start counting the days it's December
The last month of the year
The month of the birth of our saviour Christmas times
How do you spend this time?
Do you spend time with family?
Do you enjoy wrapping presents?
Do you prefer to do the cooking?
The Roasting of the turkey
Do you prefer to take a break at this time of year?
Do you enjoy the pantomimes?
Do you enjoy the Nativity plays?
Christmas times
What's your favourite thing about Christmas?
It's a time of sharing and giving
Helping the needy on our streets
Helping the older generation
Or finding time for someone that might need it
We give out toys in my church to children during the Toy
service
We give toiletries to women in the refuge
There is so much you can do during Christmas
My favourite time is the giving to the needy
What's your favourite time
Christmas times

Composed in A and E at Queens on 29/11/18
Inspired to write its Christmas time

Chocolate and Biscuits 120

It's that time of year
Our favourite snack of a lifetime
But as we become more health conscious
We no longer want to pile on the calories
But at this time of year
The supermarkets have them everywhere
They have them on display at discounted prices
They would do well as a Christmas present to a neighbour
or a church member
They have them in varieties
We have the combined biscuits and chocolate Digestives
they are called cooked chocolate biscuits
We have Quality Street Roses and Celebrations
We have Foxes,
I hope we can enjoy them both at this time of year
You can sit by the fire and enjoy a cuppa with a nice biccy
to go with it
You can have them on display during family gatherings
You can wrap them up for colleagues
You can share them with residents
But be aware you need to shed the pounds and get active
again
Chocolates and Biscuits might not be for everyone
But they are a favourite snack of a lifetime
Chocolate and Biscuits
Kit Kat, Digestives, wafers to mention but a few
I challenge you to enjoy your favourite chocolate this time of
year

*Inspired to write as I notice them on display in the shop
window*
Composed at work on 4/12/18

Shows This Time of Year 121

We enjoy the Christmas carols
Silent night
Jingle bells
O little town of Bethlehem
Ding dong merrily on high
Without programmes like X factor
It becomes boring on a Saturday night
Thank God for the jungle show
Celebrity get me out of here
The Apprentice is another one
But nothing can prepare you for the jungle
It covers everything
You can face anything
I will not question myself anymore Fleur
I overcame my fears of confined spaces Barrowman
I enjoyed the banquet Redknapp
I enjoy the trials Dec
Bush tucker trials
It's been hard I did not know what to expect Emily
It's about how you cope with the downs and come back strong
Redknapp It's an amazing show
As it showcases everything you face in Life
Your fears Your trials
Your accomplishments
Tears of Joy Feelings of desperation Hunger
Fear of heights I challenge you to go in the jungle
Like George of the jungle
You can jump out of a helicopter
You can jump out of a plane
You can go in a speed boat
The choice is yours
It is such a lifetime experience If you don't like it
Celebrity get me out of here

Inspired to write seeing the jungle show
Composed at home 8/12/2018

Reflections 122

Is a period when we reflect on where things are in our lives
Is a period when things are not going the way we expect
Reflection is a time when we consider what should have been
It is a period when we reflect on how far we have come
It's a time when we thank God for what he has done in our lives
It is a time to count our blessings and our joys
It is time to count our sorrows or sadness
It is a time to reflect on our accomplishments
It is a time to reflect on our achievements and success
It is also a time to reconsider what we can do differently
It is a time to change our approach
It is also a time to dig deeper and do some soul searching
It's also a time to reconnect with your higher God
It's a time to reconnect with families or friends if you have them
It's a time to start thinking what's next for me on my journey
Reflections makes you reposition yourself
Reflections is when you let God take the lead and direct your path
It's a time when God wants intimacy with you
Reflections

Composed in my living room
Inspired to write on the 10/12/18

Patience 123

Do you know what the word patient means?
I have learnt the meaning of the word Patience
There are similarities between Patience and patient
There are times we need to focus on the present
By doing that we learn to be patient
We cannot move before God wants us to move
God may have a plan for our life
Patient means Preparation
It means God wants you to pause and be ready for the next level
Patience is a virtue
I have heard the saying several times
I know when God wants me to wait and be patient it is for a reason
I do not rush things any longer
I wait for the right time in any situation I find my self
As I understand God will never leave you without a plan
Patience is God's plan for you
Do you remember a time you have had to be very patient on a project or a plan of yours?
I have learnt Patience on all levels
It has made me a stronger person
And Patience has measured up to Growth.
Patience is a virtue

Composed in my living room on 15/02/18
Inspired to write
following an episode
where I exercised
Patience

The Church 124

We attend Holy Cross
We also attend Good Shepherd
I attend the Kingdom Church
I used to attend the Wednesday service in Camberwell
Then I began to wonder why I had to travel to various Churches
God is one
He is invisible
He is omnipresence
He is everlasting
He is omnipotent
He is everywhere
He is the same yesterday today and forever
So, I could worship him from anywhere
I could connect with him in my spirit
I could kneel and call his name
He would hear me
I go to church to enjoy the atmosphere of togetherness
I enjoy his presence when I am singing
Singing and praising brings out the best in me
The Church is the place to be It's for weddings
It's for Baptism
It's for Confirmation
It's for everything special
It's also used for funerals
So, the church is very important to all of us
I encourage us all to keep our churches open in our communities
The church opened their doors in the winter months for the homeless
The church serves as a good community support
They provide meals at Christmas for the older generation
The Church is a focal point in our communities.

Composed in my living room on 16/12/18
Inspired to write following the Church Carol service

The Tango Tree 125

As I parked up
I looked up into the sky
There were trees in the park
Trees of different shapes
The tree with a difference
It stood tangled and represented a tango stance
It reminded me of strictly come dancing
It reminded me of dancers
Tangling
Branches tangled with one another
The beauty of dance
The beauty of nature
Brought together in a tree
Can this be untangled came to mind
Then the tree would be unwoven in love
Unwoven in nature
The Tango Tree

Composed at home on 15/07/19
Inspired to write visiting the park

What is Fear? 126

Can you accomplish fear
Can you demolish fear
Can you overpower fear
Why do you Fear
What would you lose?
Why do you worry what others may think of you?
Why do you fear the unknown?
Why do you fear to take a sideways step?
Why do you worry that you may fail or not make it?
Fear is not what we think it is
God has not given us a spirit of fear
But he has given us a spirit of peace and a sound mind
Fear is the voice of defeat trying to distract you from your goal
Fear is a distraction to your mindset
Fear is not intended for anyone
Why are you afraid of what could be?
Or what would be
Or what may be
Or what they might say
Or what would they feel
Or what if they find out that I tried
What is Fear
What is Fear to you
I hope we can demolish fear out of our minds
I hope we can overpower fear
I hope we can overshadow fear
Thou shall not Fear
Can you accomplish fear
I will fear no evil for thou art with me your rod and staff comfort me
Thou Shall not fear

Inspired to write on the train 19/12/18

It's a Time of Giving 127

It's a time of year to help the hopeless helpless
restless and needy
You can see them on the streets
In sleeping bags
Loitering in the shop doorways
They come out under the shade of the night
They beg for money on behalf of others
They knock at the door asking for a bed for the night
It's Boxing Day and they go from door to door
They approach you in the car in the gas station asking
for money to fill a Jerry can
But yet they don't have a car
You present them with a gift
But they reply they are going home to this flat
Yet it's obvious they are sleeping rough
You speak to engage them, but they prefer to be on
the streets
You offer them a hot meal but they prefer to stay
hungry but yet they need a meal
People offer them everything but there is a community
out there
They support one another yet refuse the support of a
roof over their head
It's a time of giving
Give what you can and move on
signpost and support
That's all you can do sometimes
The homeless on our streets

*Challenged to write this poem with the levels of
homelessness in our streets*

Inspired to write on 26/12/18

The Friends Catch Up 128

We went to school together
This was 40 years ago
In a boarding school for girls
We met up for a meal
It was Christmas
We connected
We spoke about our kids
We all had kids Some of us were grandmas
We thank the living Jesus
Some were single
Some were separated
Some were divorced
But we were still connected
A fight broke out in the mall
Two lads against another lad
They poured Coca Cola on him
We all were frightened
We did what any adult should do or not do
We tried to intervene
We stopped the fight
We appealed to both parties
He slammed his head against the barrier
He could have hurt him
The security men took ages to arrive on the scene
The boys did not know each other
It was an unprovoked Attack amongst black Boys
It has cost them so many lives
The violence on our streets
We stopped the fight this time We saved a life
One or two of us spoke up
Some women stopped to help the injured
What would you do?
It could be my son
It could be your son
It could be a neighbour's son
It could be a friend's son
We need to watch out for each other
The violence on our streets

I was challenged to write this poem
Having witnessed a violent attack in day light on 27/12/18
Composed on 01/01/ 2019

The Youth of Tomorrow 129

I was wondering as I walked past in the mall
I saw a sign saying youths
I stopped to see what was going on
It was a youth centre for music recording
It was opened during school time only
It was open once in a month
We have had so much stabbing on our streets
There are post code gang culture
There are issues in our communities
I just wondered why we didn't have more of these
centres in our cities
To combat the gang culture
The mayor said he has some funding
He is looking for local authorities to support him
The city of London can only do so much
With less police on our roads
The youth of tomorrow

Inspired to write seeing the youth centre
Composed on the train on 18/07/19

Ladies Night Out 130

It's the first weekend of the year
I have always enjoyed connecting with other women
To start off the year with a bang
Ladies together under one roof
Dancing singing rejoicing praising worshipping dining
All dressed up in the finest of finest
Hair all done up
Wigs hair pieces
Hands Manicured women pamper themselves all to look
good in the presence of God our maker
You want to be at your best
You want to be looking your best
The freedom in expression is amazing
Ladies just feel comfortable
Without any men in the room
You could sense the joy and it was just a time to let go of
any worries
To let go of any anxiety
To let go any hindrances
You let go of any barriers
I want to associate with Ladies Refresh groups
I want to associate with Webinars
I want to associate with groups that promote growth
Groups that promote well being
Groups that promote self-care
The Ladies night out
First Saturday of the year is called
Dining with Christ
I start my year with this for the last four years
And it's been Great
I have gone on to achieve my goals

Inspired to write following our DWC event
Composed on 07/01/19

The Challenge of Writing 131

I give God the glory
He is the beginning and the end
He gives wisdom and tells you what to do when you don't
know what to do
It's like a blank canvas
Let your thoughts flow
Don't force it
Let it come out like a stream of water
It flows wherever it wants to go
I often ponder I let God lead my thoughts
There are days the ideas come and if you don't jot it down
It goes like a game
So, I jot things down sometimes in my notes
I look at events affecting us globally
I listen to the news and try to make sense of it
I find it intriguing how God let's it flow out of Me
I am grateful for the opportunity to be able to story tell
I received an email from the writer's club today
My creative writing group I joined on Boxing Day
I am grateful for joining the poetry community to share some
of my poems
I am grateful for YouTube to be able to recite my poems
I am grateful for Facebook and the networking across the
globe
The challenges of writing are great if you open your mind to
receive
I challenge you to open your mind
Pick up a pen and flow with it
The challenge of writing

*Inspired to write after receiving a breakthrough
today on my book*

Composed in my living room 09/01/19

Gratitude 2018 132

What are you grateful for?
Attended the Refresh session today
An opportunity to network with other ladies
Trying to do things in my local community
Trying to network in my local church
Mention one thing you are grateful for
Around the table I started writing poetry in May
I had my grandson after eight years
I got engaged in January and got married in August
My son went diving and caught an infection but thank
God he is healed
My husband had an operation and has healed
I had an argument with my brother after six years healing
We thank God for our homes, water and food
We thank God for our Children
My daughter is a policewoman and I pray for her daily
When things affect our children, it cuts deep into you
It's good to share I am glad to have Jesus
Deception stops you from being your self
I went to Ireland on vacation
I spent time in our friend's holiday home
Our neighbour's daughter got married
I completed the Alpha Course
I lost my son 4 years ago, but I have now accepted
There is no situation that God can't help you
My granddaughter who is twelve moved in with me
God is faithful
I am a childminder with a troubled childhood I am giving back
We should hold on to Gods promises God knows our situations
God knows all our hopes
Issues of creativity, healing acceptance, Hope, protection, promises,
giving back and receptions
I was inspired to write this poem making sense of the Refresh
session
It was inspiring how threads of life came together from one session
I challenge you to show gratitude and see what amazing things can
be construed

Composed in my living room on 12/01/18

The Local Theatre 133

Situated in the beautiful town of Brentwood
On the outskirts of Essex
We took a drive up the A127
On my way from the Audi car shop
It was my younger son's 25th birthday
We arrived at a beautiful relaxing town
Full of nice shops on the high road
We saw the yellow building after the small roundabout
It was the theatre
The Brentwood Theatre
It was their 25th celebration anniversary
They were having an open day for the locals
We joined the Tour guide
We were shown round the theatre
We met the different groups that run shows in the theatre
We were taken round the crew rooms where all the
equipment was stored
We went to the prop rooms and saw all the costumes on
display
We went behind the stage and saw all the Victorian artefacts
and furniture
We went behind the scenes to see all the lighting equipment
The voice over demonstrations
It was a place of beauty
It was a place of creativity
We saw so many families with children visiting the theatre
It was a nice atmosphere
I was offered the opportunity to volunteer
I wanted to book a show for my birthday
It was the open day in my local theatre
There is so much to do in Brentwood
I would go back there for more fun

*I was challenged to write following my visit to the local
theatre
Composed in my living room on 12/01/18*

My Day in Covent Garden 134

It was my birthday
I woke up feeling quite numb
I had been looking forward to my day
But when the day arrived
I had received calls from Nigeria
I had messages from friends around the globe
I had a flash back of my late parents
They were both in heaven look Looking down at me
As I sat on the train
I pondered a bit as I looked through the window
A thought occurred to me I
Could sit and ponder all day long
It would not make a difference
So, I shook my self-off this negative thought
Thought of the birthday cake I got for my colleagues at work
Thought of my day ahead of me
I was going to Covent Garden for the day
I had no plan but was faithful
That once I got there God will work out something for me
I had to trust him
My hubby had gone ahead and was waiting for me as I came out of the station
He is my everything
He is my everything
I thank God for the gift of life
And thank God for my life
Happy birthday to me
My day in Covent Garden
Thankful for all the messages I received on my birthday

Inspired to write following my birthday
Composed in my living room on 18/01/19

Snow Sleet 135

As I came out of the station
I waited at the bus stop for my bus 294
It's due in 6 minutes
As I queue to get on the bus
I observe the sleet coming down
It's our first snow of the year
As I sit on the bus
The man next to me an elder gentleman is happy asking
me it's snowing
Yes, the snow has come down upon us in mighty thuds
The lady asks him if the snow fall will set
The snow creates conversation on the bus
Otherwise everyone remains quiet
I say to the older man be careful when you get off the bus
I am only going to the pub across the road
The weather can create conversations amongst us
Some come out for a chat
Some have no one to talk to all day
This might be the only conversation of the day
The Snow conversations
The weather conversations
Conversations on the bus
The snow can open doors for others
Snow sleet
Snowflakes
Snow fall

*I was challenged to write this poem having witnessed our
first snow of the year*

Composed to write 22/02/19

The Love Couple 136

I sat on the train
I was on my way to Romford
It was my daughters open day
I observed the young couple
Love was in the air
They were into each other
They looked into each other's eyes
She was playing on her phone
He was stroking her hair
She would lean into him
There was a young girl sitting opposite her
There was a man in the corner opposite him
They were oblivious to people around them
The couple were in a world of their own
The train stopped The young girls mum pulled her up
She stood and looked at the couple
She must have been mesmerised by their actions
The young lady smiled back at her Her mum took her off the train
I noticed the young man opposite them changed his seat
There was an older man reading a paper sitting behind the
young couple People getting on with their own business
The young couple stood out amongst the crowd
They were happy
They were carefree in nature The young girl could identify
She probably wondered what she was missing
Could not understand why her mum was not like that
She seemed to wonder why the other passengers were so
serious The love couple on the train Made me think
We are all busy in our own worlds And need to take a moment to
stop and enjoy what is around us In the present moment
Just like the little girl did Next time you are on the train
Enjoy the moment The Love couple got off the stop before me
The Love Couple on the train ...

I was inspired to write this poem having witnessed a couple in
love I hope we can love ourselves first in other to share love with
others around us

Composed 24/01/19 in my living room

The Happy Team 137

I was attending a cousin's birthday party
We drove up the M6 to Manchester
We arrived at our destination after a four-hour
eventful drive
We were too early to check in
We arrived at the reception and were met by a
young sharp looking young man
He asked us to return in two hours
Our room was not ready
So, he offered us a drink in the bar on the other side
of the hotel
The Manchester Bar
He was chilled pleasant and remarkable
It struck my attention as it is not very common that
staffs are happy doing what they do
It would be nice to know what makes their team tick
We arrived for the breakfast the following morning
We were met by another young lad
He welcomed us and asked if we had breakfast
there before
He explained it was buffet style and feel free to help
ourselves
We had a nice meal in the breakfast area
The lady was singing as she cleared the plates
She came up to ask if we enjoyed our meal
If there was anything, she could do for us
She was pleasant and entertaining
It was the Holiday Inn Team
They were unique, dynamic and creative
The happy team

I was inspired to write as I received excellent
customer service during my stay at Manchester

Composed in the car on 27/01/19

The Bridge on the A1 138

On our journey home
It was very windy
We could feel the wind blowing
Under the car
On the windows
In all directions
It was cold
It was freezing, but warm at the same time
We arrived at the junction of the A1
As I looked to the left
I noticed a bridge
It was full of arcs underneath
With a stream flowing below
It reminded me of a journey I took to New York
The bridge was a breath of fresh air
On a long journey on a windy cold day
It connected two towns
It led from the left to the right
It was one-way cause
The cars had to give way to each other
It was a breath of fresh air
Compared to the traffic on the motorway
I felt a feeling of relaxation overwhelm me
I wonder what it was called
So, I decided to give it a name to remind me of my
journey
The Bridge on the A1
When next you're on a journey
Remember to take in the moments you come across
To the left or to your right
It's all worth it in the end

*I was inspired to write following the sitting of the Bridge
on the A1*
Composed in the car on 27/01/19

The Painting in the Mirror on the Wall 139

The fish restaurant
We had been there a year ago
It was our annual review
We were referred there by our social worker Jackie
I had my CQC interview in the fish restaurant
It was remarkable for me
We had just left the panel and decided to stop by
We ordered our meal and were waiting
I noticed the picture on the wall
There were two of a kind by the same artist
As I sat, I observed the picture was in the mirror
A lady sat and was waiting for a friend
She joined our photo
As I took a photo of the painting in the mirror
I thought it looked beautiful on its own
And even more creative in the mirror
The lady was caught up in our photo
Fortunately, she was asked to join us for the meal
The picture in the mirror
I decided to write a poem about my photo

I was inspired to write this poem having looked at my picture
I encourage you to take in your surroundings wherever you are

Benidorm 140

We wanted a short break
It was bitter cold in London
We booked our flights and off we went
We prayed for journey mercies
We thank God for a safe arrival
It was a bumpy ride towards Benidorm
We saw the mountains from the air
The Sea was blue
The skyscrapers from the distance
The lovely Levante beach I heard so much about
A distance of just over two hours
Made a huge difference
Temperatures of -2 to highs of 25
I was amazed as I dropped my case
Had some lunch and headed into town
The hotel two doors from us I stopped for a photo
Sol Pelicanos Benidorm
We headed to the Benidorm market
We headed to the Levante Beach
We met a guy with an umbrella hat singing a lovely tune he
invited us to join in
We missed our way on our first night
But were fortunate to find the city bus tour
It was an amazing first day in Benidorm
We arrived back at our hotel for a long but relaxing night
We were in Benidorm.

Inspired to write following my first day in Benidorm
Written on the coach to Valencia 31/02/19

The Tour Guide 141

We were booked to go to Valencia
We arrived at the coach stop
The coach had not arrived
We bumped into another couple
We were going to Valencia
The coach arrived
The gentleman with a cap
He had an American accent
I asked if he was American
He said no I am not from Trumps country
We sat on the coach
It was full of passengers
He spoke about his wife being English from Yorkshire a town called Doncaster
He was half Californian after all
He gave out some information
He came up to me and asked if I was American
It's good to mix and mingle
As you never know who you could bump into
It's nice to be good to people
He enjoyed what he did for a living
He gave us enough information to get us by in Valencia
But most importantly he was our tour guide for the day, and he made it clear
He was working for us
I like that part of the Tour guide
He was fantastic

I was inspired to write this poem in the coach on the way to Valencia as I enjoyed the conversation of the Tour guide
Composed on 31/01/19

Valencia 142

The third largest town in Spain
We stopped at La Sofar for a coffee break
We drove past Colleen the town with 52 acres of land for rice plantation
A bit of history around Virgin Mary
Surrounded by 40 different types of oranges
Growing on trees in every corner
We arrived in Valencia
It was full of Roman artefacts and history
The pavements were made from marble of the highest quality stone
We sat for a chat at Five Guys
We went into town through the narrow Spanish streets
We set off through the homeless alleys where we saw a lot of beggars
I take a photo with a statue in gold
I bought a magnet from the gentleman on the roadside
We drove past the mountains
We drove past the coliseum
We arrived at the cathedral the biggest church in Spain
We arrived at the water fountain fall in the square
It was an amazing site with lots of tourists
My highlight was the indoor market
Where we got to meet the locals and I bought a guitar as a souvenir
The Roman culture was amazing in a Spanish town
It made me wonder how we get to make impressions on others
You could sense the Romans within the architecture of the Colosseum building in the town
Valencia

I was challenged to write this poem following a visit to Valencia the third largest city in Spain
Composed on the 31/01/2019

The Fish Town Calpe 143

We arrived at the sea front
We saw the fish nets by the beach
The fishermen were tying up their nets
The Sea was rough
We arrived at the fish restaurant
There were different fish on display
I went for sole and salmon
He went for tilapia
The fish was cooked to order
The staff served us a glass of Sangria
We waited for half an hour
The fish was cooked to perfection
It was grilled and seasoned well
The oil was of the nicest quality
There was a beautiful painting that caught my attention
It was hanging on the wall
The more customers that came in, they made their orders
We were served fish that was caught on the day
I bought two magnets and a necklace too
To remind me of my visit to Calpe
I understand the Spanish served the best meals as it was
always served fresh
I enjoyed my day in Calpe a small
Fish town off the coast of Benidorm

*I was inspired to write this poem having enjoyed a fish dish
at the fish town of Calpe*
Composed in the hotel reception in Benidorm on 01/02/19

The Universal Painting Caught My Attention 144

The painting was hanging on the wall
Just above our table in the fish restaurant
It was the only one in the room
The black woman with a band
The piano in a twisted staircase brought music to my heart
The coloured flowers in the painting reminded me of the colours of life
The painting had so much meaning
I kept watching it while I was having my meal
The different meanings of life could mean so much to anyone
We are all on this journey twisting here and there
We are all listening to music and have our different favourites
Jazz, hip-hop, reggae and all what not
We love our different colours Red, Green, yellow and
all what not We like our different flowers
Daffodils, Roses, blueberries and all what not
What is the meaning of life?
We are all on a twisted but colourful journey
We must make meaning of the different colours
We must make meaning of the different music
We must make meaning of the different flowers
The diverse women in life
She reminds me of the universe
We are all but one person on a colourful twisted journey in life
It could be musical, colourful or a twisted journey
It depends on what you make of it
You could be black You could be white
But it is one colourful twisted journey
What is your journey looking like?
Colourful?
Musical?
Flowery?
Black or white?
Twisted or straight?

I was inspired to write looking at this painting in the fish restaurant
Composed in my hotel in Benidorm on 02/02/19

The Beach Walk- Mother and Baby 145

We sat and were looking up at the blue sky
It was just after breakfast and we took a five-minute stroll
The beach was packed with tourists
We were amazed with the number of vacationers and the locals
We decided to sit and watch the sea for a moment
As we sat at the Tiki beach bar
I noticed the gorilla in the garden she was carrying her baby
She reminded me of my daughter at home
I remembered how the bible teaches us that even the birds of the air
The lord will take care of them talk less of you and me
If a gorilla could take care of her baby
If animals have the natural instinct to take care of their own
We notice there were loads of beggars by the sea front
We were warned that the system takes care of them and we are not obliged to assist them
The interesting part is do we humans help each other enough
Do we protect each other like the mother gorilla was protecting her baby?
The white woman sitting in front of Sol Pelicanos Benidorm
The lady in front of the church in Valencia
The man sitting in front of Don Pacho hotel
There are so many that come to mind
We should love and protect each other
The beach walk mother and baby sent a gentle reminder to us all
To love our neighbour as ourselves
The beach walk mother and baby sat in the garden of Tiki Beach as a gentle reminder to us all on vacation and beyond
Spread the news

Inspired to write having seen the mother gorilla and her baby
Composed in my hotel in Benidorm on 03/02/19

The Table Aquarium 146

I was looking forward to my second creative writing class
I arrived at the library
I went upstairs
I went to the reception and then realised it was
Wednesday
My class was on Thursday
I sat at the reception
I observed the table behind me
It was an Aquarium
Never seen one like it before
It was interesting as I just returned from Benidorm
It reminded me of the beach in a tank
It was relaxing as I swiped my hand across the surface
There were little pink fish
Stones or pebbles, rocks and plants
There was everything to remind me of a vacation
I felt so relaxed and thought I would write a poem about
the Table Aquarium
I did not know the right word to describe
What I had experienced
But it made sense to write about The Table Aquarium in
the library
When next you're in your local library
Check out what things of interest you may find
Who knows?

*Inspired to write following my visit to the library for my
creative writing class*
Composed in the bus on 07/02/19

The Beautiful Gates of Benidorm 147

They reminded me of a time I was vacating
I would enter his gates with thanksgiving in my heart
I will enter his gates with praise
Anywhere I looked I observed gates of different designs
On the beach front of Levante beach
On the side roads of Mediterráneo
On the streets on the way to Highlands of Altea
This is where the celebrities live behind these beautiful gates
I understand the Russian prime minister built a gold monarch surrounded by
gates for his mother
There was a lot of history behind these gates
Gates serve as doors to our prayers
Gates in the city serve as doors for God to come into our cities
So, if we look at gates, we should pay them our attention
As they prevent burglars or intruders from coming into our homes
Also you need to open your gate to let your guests in
Also we need to open our thoughts for greater ideas
Also we need to open our minds for the love of God to flow into
our hearts if we look at Gates, they could mean a lot, bring a lot
to mind the red gate I saw on the sea front of Levante beach
A lady came out of the apartment on to the seafront
on to the beach walk and straight on to the beach
It made such a difference to see one of the gates in action
Which reminds me to say when one gate shuts another gate
opens each time you see a gate don't just walk past it
Remind yourself of the beauty of gates in our lives
And what they could mean to us and beyond that what they
might mean in the spiritual realm
It might be a good idea to leave a gate open
And it might not be such a great idea to keep your gate locked
So, what would you do?
It's best to enter the gate with an open mind with thanksgiving in
our hearts I would enter his gates with praise

I was inspired to write having observed a number of gates in Benidorm
Composed in my bedroom on 11/02/19 started on 10/02/19

Valentine 148

What does the word Valentine mean?
Why do we celebrate Valentine's day on Feb. 14th each year?
Do you look forward to Valentine's Day?
Do you love yourself as you love others?
The word of God says
Love your neighbour as your self. I went to a boarding School
We had a tree that grew every year and around this time
Students would pluck the flowers and present it to one another
It's interesting how the tradition of Valentine is celebrated
across the globe. We buy flowers, chocolates, teddy bears
and present them to loved ones. Do we love ourselves as
others love us? Valentine's Day is also called St Valentine's
Day. It is also known as the feast of Valentine
It is a day set aside to send a card to someone you are
connected to romantically
It is also known for the celebration of love and affection
The first Valentine's Day was in 496
It is part of a Roman festival and has its origins in Christianity
The Romans had a festival called Lupercalia that was
celebrated in the middle of February
I hope we can continue to celebrate the month of love with our
loved ones around us. We can remember our loved ones on
days like this. We can find love on days like this
There is so much love in the atmosphere on a day like this
Love is in the air, everywhere when I look around
I hope we can all tap into love and energy in the atmosphere
and spread it around. I received love today in the card shop
Which was an interesting act
The lady said, I hope you go off and celebrate Valentine's Day
with your husband. She bought a card, a balloon and a
bouquet of flowers.The shops were packed with lovers
Purchasing cards for their loved ones, as that is the
significance of St Valentine's Day. Happy Valentine's Day to
everyone experiencing love today.

*I was inspired to write this poem as I had been celebrating
Valentine's Day this season. I was challenged to write this
poem on 14/02/19 having received a lot of love from my hubby
as always, It's a nice feeling to feel loved and be loved*

Silence 149

It's ever so quiet on the trains
On my way home from a long day at work
I can see the faces of the passengers
Some of them frowning
No smiles on the train
Some have headphones on listening to music
Some are reading a book
Some are not making eye contact
It makes me wonder what goes on in their minds
I am not any different
But I try to focus my attention
I try to write about the situation
I try to make sense of events around me
I try to take in the here and now
I was speaking to a colleague
He is writing his own book he told me
He felt the same way too
It's interesting what goes on in life
It's interesting what life does not prepare us for
The silence can be captivating
The silence can be mind blowing
Let's make use of the silence on our trains
Next time you are faced with silence
Make use of the opportunity
It's okay to be still in the moment
The silence on our trains

Composed on the 21/02/19 on the train. I was
challenged to write after experiencing moments of
silence on our trains

My Mother 150

Today I celebrate you
In all happiness and thinking of you
As a mum that took all her time to care from the
Genuine strength of your heart
A strong woman
A grandmother, mother in law
A socialite in her lifetime
The Yeyemeso of Idanre Land
Fashion was your second nature
You loved your colours
I remember your laughter, your sense of humour, your
dedication to your community
I remember your love for your family and friends
You left a legacy for us to walk into
You left so soon
You loved your church and your society
Trying to bring everyone together
Nothing was too big for you to accomplish
You were dedicated and loyal to your friends and family
My friends knew you as a firm but loving mother
You were always there to celebrate any milestones or
achievements
We celebrate you today as we mark the 13th year of
your anniversary
Without you has been a huge gap which only God can
fill
We thank God for your life
As we celebrate your anniversary today Mum
Rest on Yeyemeso of Idanre Land
We miss you we love you
Goddy and Binah with love always.

Composed on the 13th Anniversary of my late mum
Composed on 23/02/19 at home.

The Librarian 151

She was amazing
She was helpful
She always wore her heart on her sleeves
She had a smile on her face
She was always there to assist
Nothing was too much or too big for her to accomplish
I went in the library for six months
She would always ask how you were feeling on the day
When I had not been for a while
She would say I have not seen much of you lately
She would make you feel welcome
She acted as if she knew you personally
She enjoyed her role
She was the Librarian
She deserved to be the staff of the month
She congratulated me when I told her I got a job
She assisted me when the computers froze at times
She helped to put a book on reserve
She would help with scanning the books out
She would help with putting the books on the shelves
She would help with photocopying
She would also ensure everyone in the library was safe
She maintained order in the library at all times
She was firm but fair to all
She was approachable
The Librarian

Composed at the Love of Libraries Worksop
on 28/02/19
Inspired to write as part of the Word Festival

The Swimming Pool 152

I was attending a wedding
On the deck top
We congregated for drinks and canapés
It was a beautiful day
We had a three-course meal
They had to rearrange the room
We had a coffee and some biscuits
As I stood waiting for the fireworks display
I noticed some vacationers
It was the Carbis Bay hotel
There was a small pool on the side
With children having fun
Families relaxing on deck chairs
The shape of the pool was different
It caught my attention
So, I wrote a poem about the swimming pool
Have you seen any pool with a peculiar shape?

Inspired to write following a wedding in Cornwall
Composed on the train Inspired to write having
seen the pool on 25/07/19

The Kayak 153

We stopped at one of the services
We were on our way to Cornwall for a wedding
A lady stopped to take a photo
I came out of the car to do the same
We smiled at each other
She said she was using her photo for snap chat
I said I was going to write a poem
She said we could both pretend
We were going on the Kayak
I asked what it was called
She said a kayak
When I arrived on the beach
I saw so many kayaks on the beach in Carbis Bay
The kayak
Have you sailed on a Kayak before?

Composed on the train 25/07/19
Inspired to write having seen a kayak

A Love of Libraries, Books and Wonderful Words 154

A library in a tree
A book on a free
A library on an elephant
Is one I would like to see
A library on the beach
Is never out of reach
A library full of food
Is one that's nice and good
A library full of books
Is one that's full of looks
A library with science fiction
Is one that's full of attraction
A library with Languages
Is one full of knowledge?
A library with literates
Is one full of wisdom?
A library with wisdom
Is one full of words?
A book on Shakespeare
Would open doors for fears
A library on a boat
Is one full of float?
A library on a truck
Is one on a truck
A library in a booth
Is one put on hold?
A library in a grave
Is one full of bravery?
A poem full of words
Is one play on words

Composed at the library event in Newham competition
Inspired to write following my attendance at the
Newham library festival

The Tree House on the Foot Bridge 155

It was our staff annual conference
We met up at the Bishops gate pub for breakfast
We were having a fun day
I stopped to take photos of the sites
We walked past lots of wonderful architectural buildings
I was having fun
My colleague asked don't you come up to London that
much
I do not take life too seriously
My eyes caught the attention of the footbridge in the
middle of London
There was a tree house on the footbridge
It looked amazing
It was lying at an angle
I was not sure if you could walk through the house on the
bridge
My imagination crept in
I wondered what it stood for
I was quite curious to know
And then I thought I would write a poem about the
The tree on the foot bridge
Hope it has inspired you as much as it has inspired me

Composed on the train on 08/03/19
Inspired to write having seen this on my way to our
annual conference

Women's Day 156

Memories bring you out
Marching is in unison
Voicing is being heard
Independence means everything
Leverage means fairness
Togetherness means unity
Unity is power
Victory is amazing
United we are Victorious
Nations make the world

Inspired to write following Women's day

Believe 157

I can't do this
I am not used to doing it this way
But you can try and see if it works
I am not sure if this will work
You are nobody
Who told you it might work?
Or it may work
Even if you try
You are a failure
No one has done this and made it work
Why do you think you are any different?
I am me and I am not a failure
I am willing to give this a try
I am doing my best I think
I am trying to use the first voice here
I will start with a letter
I will move with a word
I will continue with a sentence
I will write a paragraph
I will write a sonnet
I will publish a book
I have done it
Who said I can't do this?
Listen to that voice in your head
Believe in your own strength
Believe in your own abilities
I can do this

*Composed at the Pen to write workshop
on 09/03/18
Inspired to write in First voice*

Life is a Journey 158

From East to West
From North to South
Who are we to challenge the divine being?
The maker of heaven and earth
He directs our paths
He takes us on an unending journey
Called Life
We do not know the beginning
We do not know the end
We must give up to him
It's an amazing journey if you can
He opens doors, no one can shut
He goes before you
When you don't know, he tells you what to do
He has unfinished business with everyone
Life is a journey

Inspired to write at the Pen to write workshop
Composed on 09/03/19

The Spice (Smell Speed Writing) 159

The scent from the orange powder in the bottle
was different
The Spice reminded me of making a curry An
ingredient
The floral beauty was inviting to the eye to the
nose
My five senses to play
I felt like tasting with my mouth
The aroma was a natural feel which was not
overpowering
The beauty of writing from a smell was
unfamiliar
But I was inspired to give it a try
The smell of curry is one that's interesting
amongst other poets
Words like Spicy, flowery, aroma, cooking,
texture, orangy, feeling aura come to mind
My five senses are challenged by this spice
Seeing, smelling, tasting, touching and
perhaps listening
The Spice

*Composed at the Growing Poetry workshop at
the National poetry library
Inspired to write on 17/03/19*

My Shadow 160

What would happen if I didn't have a shadow?
What would that mean if I was in the sun
What could that mean if I missed my own shadow
Would I have one in the rain
Could I have one that looked at me
Would I have one taller or shorter
My Shadow is me
If no one has told you so
It can't be anyone else
My Shadow is different to yours
My Shadow would only leave when I am gone
When I am no more
When I am laying in the coffin
I guess I would know no different
My Shadow could actually follow me down below
Who knows I have never been there?
I play games with my Shadow
When it's sunny
Or when I am taking a selfie
I don't want it to appear
My Shadow can only be me
My height
My weight
My moves
My Shadow is always on the floor
It's never above
When I move to the right it's there
When I move to the left it's there
When I stand still it's there
When will it go away?
It would only leave me when I am gone
When I am no more
My Shadow

Inspired to write in the Growing Poetry Workshop
Composed at the National Poetic Library on 17/03/19

The Dome Rooftop 161

It stood tall in the centre garden
In the enclosed gardens of Bethlehem
The roofs pointed towards the blue sky
The windows all shaped in a triangle
The roofs were designed that way for a reason
Most churches have the same roof design
The windows with artefacts of bible stories
The ceiling telling a story of baby Jesus
The dome in the middle was an attraction
For tourists visiting Jerusalem
The birthplace of our saviour
It caught my attention as I stood tall
It was inviting to the eye
The roof top shaped like a dome

*Composed in the Growing Poetry workshop
on 17/03/19
Inspired to write from an Architecture prompt
Challenge
Started in Stratford and ended up in Bethlehem
Keep it up and mix up the ideas*

*Composed in Bethlehem on my journey to Israel
Inspired to write having sighted the dome in
Israel*

Anti-Hate 162
World Poetry Day

Comes in different shapes and forms
Don't give in to it
Don't put up with it
Are you dealing with your own battle?
Everyone has battles in life
Are you looking for a way out?
Trust God as he will make a way
Are you feeling stuck and it shows up in Hate?
Crime Anger, Hate, Dislikes, Disengagement,
Negativity
Hatred
Unhappiness
Because you can't control how you feel
You can't find a way out
You take it out on others
You try and form an army to follow you
Yesterday was world Happiness day
Do you feel it
Do you see it
I put up a Happiness index last year
But this year i didn't bother
You must walk your own race
Anti-Hate
Don't put up with it
Don't give in to it
Say something today
You could be Helping someone today

Composed on my journey to work
Inspired to write after Happiness Day on 21/03/19

The Tulips in Reception 163

The end of year party
It was at the golf club
We were there the year before
We arrived through the side door
But this time we were late
So, we took the reception
The centre table was made from oak
The staircase was on the left which took us to the
reception room
The Tulips stood tall in the centre of the room
It was welcoming and relaxing at the same time
I stood and watched them
It was a touch of nature in the most unusual places
I remembered the year before they had some form of
decor
The Tulips reminded me of bringing the outdoor into the
indoor
It was inviting on the eye
It was beautiful on the eye
It made you relax while you waited to be called
I took a picture to remind me
The Tulips in reception
When next you are out take in the environment
Think about the beauty and aura that transforms the
room

Composed on the train on 25/03/19
Inspired to write following an outing over the weeks

The Planters on the Dance Floor 164

Reminded me of my planter on my kitchen window
They were beauty on the dance floor
What a difference it made to the room
What an unusual place to display a gorgeous planter
Then it occurred to me the room doubles up as an
evening room during the day and a disco hall at night
Once you added the disco flooring it transformed the room
With the dim lights you would forget where you were
As you walked past you could not miss the gorgeous
looking leaves
They were green and hard been pruned to the highest
standards
They had been pruned from the heart
The planter has been watered from the heart
It had spread its wings in such a way that looked graceful
to see
The leaves were healthy looking
I would encourage you to take care of your self
Just as the golf club had pruned its planter for all to see
The planter was on display by the walkway
It could not be missed but I guess
I took a picture to remind me of the Planter on the disco
floor
I looked at the planter as I danced away on the floor
Enjoy your dance on the floor and remember to take care
of yourself and water the Planter on your way out.
The planter on the dance floor.

Composed at home on 26/03/2019
Inspired to write having seen the planter on the dance
floor at the golf club

The Beast in Cyberspace 165

"Log off Delete"
I did once ask people to delete themselves
off from my page
"There's no worth there"
Is really strange I hear
"To search for reason"
Is like asking for treason
"Through high-speed fibre "
Is like high street drama
"Honestly don't waste your time"
It's apparent people like you but pretend not to
"If you crave freedom of speech"
It's right that you allow people to be reached
"I'd mute the beast and then block his mates"
I would carry on as if we were mates
"Through curation, less grief associates"
Through association, add brief friendships
"The beast that lives in cyberspace"
Is what makes the world go around
"Does not care whose life's consumed"
Is why Instagram has been construed
"It scares and lies, dividing us "
It's truth and unity, binding us
"It laughs then retweets hate as bait "
She cries then scars herself as hate
"Get a life, outside phones and screen"
Is why Facebook monitors our screen time
"Weight of responsibility breaks "
The right of our ability freaks
The beast in Cyberspace.

*Composed in the Barking Foxes Split poem Poetry
group on 30/03/19
Copyrights by Sarah Reeson
Poetry News (Winter 2018)*

Team Workshop 166

The day arrived at last Our Team Workshop
The flip chart up The felt pens in various colours
The Team members on their way
The first quarter of the year The various contributions
The learning experiences
Our short comings and short talks
Our problems solved by numbers
Our questions answered through solving
We won the residents inclusion league.
We had a half-day session on site
Reflection on our practice was great With builders and
painters on site
But it was still a success despite the odds
The residents cooperation on the day
The staff turn up a bit late The catering done to time
All tasks delegated performed
RBM attends and all questions answered
We had bowling at the all stars Two groups of four
It was a time for Team bonding All eight of us stuck our
backs into it There was laughter and fun
We did not take ourselves too seriously
There were players with different strengths
That's what it's all about Teamwork makes the dream work
We had players with different abilities
That's what it's all about
Supporting each other towards a common goal
We played one game and then it was time to go
We joked and smiled and felt more at ease with each other
Our Team Workshop
We had a meal at the Turkish restaurant
A time to relax and share ideas
It worked so well, and we talked over lunch
What brought us together was the passion and values we
shared for our work
The responses and Learning experience
Teamwork makes the dream work

Composed on the train following our workshop 04/04/19
Inspired to write following our workshop

Sky is the Limit 167

Look up and what do you see
The blue the white or what might be
The night the stars or what time it might be
The clouds the rain or the sunshine
The Sky is the not the limit
It depends on how you see it
The extra mile you take can make you stronger
When you look up imagine you are in space
The astronauts and the planets
The air space station are things that interest me
Space is amazing from what I see
The many times you are afloat
With little and have not much to eat
The funny suits you must wear to make you safe
The astronauts must do loads to survive
How can sky be the limit
With all these other planets
Neptune Jupiter and Saturn
How can sky be the limit as there is life outside of
earth, we've been told
Sky is the limit if you see it so
I would want to go beyond the sky one day
Sky is the limit if you are career minded
Sky is the limit if you are working on a project
Sky can be the limit if you don't stretch your self
I would imagine Sky as a stepping stone for more
The achievers must look beyond the sky and tell me
what you see
Is Sky the limit?

*Composed following my creative writing workshop on
02/04/19*
Inspired to write about my Chosen topic

Acrostic Poetry 168

Air quality is not great on an Aeroplane
Energy levels can sometimes feel depleted
Rise to the challenge with a glass of water
Optimism is great when you are flying
Planning ahead is great so you don't miss your flight
Landing safe should be your main objective
Attention to detail for the Pilot is a must
Never give up on Hope during your flight
Exercise is a great way of enduring your flight

Timing is great when you're catching the train
Right on board in the right cabin/ drain
Arriving safe at your destination /train
Interconnecting on the Eurostar/ Train is great
Night-time travel is best in case it rains
Busking on the top deck in New York
Universal studios in Florida
Sleeping in paradise

Growing Poetry workshop on 14/04/2019
Inspired to write a mode of transport from
Acoustic poetry

Stereoscopic Object Poetry 169

Left eye views
Right eye views
The same image in a 3D dimension
I guess it depends on what you see
I guess it depends on the image
I guess it depends on the angle you view it from
I guess it depends on how you see it, or view it
I guess we can see different things
I guess we are all different
We may use the same stethoscope
But the image again may appear different
From what he sees, what she sees or what they see or
what I see
The Stethoscope image might be clear, blurry, static, in
motion
Not sure what you might see
Not sure what she may see
Not sure what they could see
We could get in the same car, yet perceive a different
journey
We could buy the same book and interpret the story
differently
We could buy the same drink and yet get a different taste
We could take the same topic and yet write a different
story
It depends on the perspective
No two views are the same
No two rivers are the same

Composed at Growing Poetry on 11/04/2019
Inspired to write using an object.

Seasons 170

Spring is upon us
The beautiful daffodils that form a flower bed
As we drive on the motorway from Calais
The beautiful yellow springs upon us
The motorway is blossoming on both sides that I look
It lengthens as it stretches across the lawn of green
that overlook the hills
The blue skies above with a Yellow carpet below
The smell is beautiful and the colour yellow springs to
mind
The yellow lawn is no respecter of Sheep, Rabbits or
horses
The spring colour that litters the shops
With Easter chicks hatching from yellow eggs
The season of spring brings so much life to it
The Easter card I received is sprung with yellow
daffodils across the front
The beauty of yellow surrounds us
The season of springs signifies Growth
New life Hatching and new beginnings
As we are surrounded by Eggs which brings new life
Spring is a season of growth

Composed in my apartment in France on 17/04/19
Inspired to write for the Spring Open mic competition

Windmill 171

The beauty of the windmill
They stood tall in the highway
Each with a three-way mechanism
Each with a stalk as tall as a kite
Each one painted in grey
They seem small from a distance
When seen in a group
They served a purpose of providing energy which
became light
Light in turn which is used in our households
There is so much that windmills do across nations
They are erected on our highways
Or in remote areas as they take up so much space
I have driven past these many times on my way to Paris
or Le Marnee
But this day was different
I thought I could write about the Windmills on the way to
Le Marnee
I would encourage you to look left on your way to Paris
from Calais
As they cannot be missed
They are tall and still
They move so slowly you can count their blades
They are very huge when you come close to them but
very small from
A distance
The streams flow by
They grass is greener on the other side
The hills in the distance
The windmills stand strong in rain or shine
The windmills stand strong providing us with light
The windmills are a view to see
The Windmills on the highway

Inspired to write on my way to Le Marnee
Composed in my apartment in France on 19/04/2019

The Golf Course 172

As I wake up
I open the blinds and what do I see
The green grass stretching across the lawns
The view of golfers walking across the terrain
What a lovely view to be woken by
Pushing their buggy across the holes
A view that is welcoming
The golfers enjoy the weather
A sky that's blue from the horizon
The halls are strewn across the valleys
The lakes are unassuming
The balls are dug deep into the grass
The streams flow by without the ducks
The groups of golfers enjoying a game
The swans dominate the lake
The scenery is one of amazement
The Golf course is an interesting topic of
discussion
But the Golfers play on in Bailly-Romainvilliers
Come rain or shine
It's a beautiful sight to start my day especially on a
sunny day
The Golf course

Composed in my Villa in France on 23/04/19
Inspired to write with the view in site

The Black Power Bike 173

It was curvy
It was strong
It is fast
It is beautiful
It was a charmer
It is my neighbour's bike
He is a courier
He would storm off in the early hours
He would be back by midday
He would park it on the drive
But this day it was parked on the street
As I took a walk
I noticed it on my way
I decided to write a poem
About the black bike
The black power bike
My neighbour's bike
Inspired to write seeing the bike in the drive

Composed in the car on my way
to Wales

The Mystery Pair 174

We went on our morning walk
We took a right turn
We ended up on the roundabout
We could see the Radisson hotel
The two ducks were sitting on the grass
They seemed content and did not budge
I moved closer and attempted to talk but they
did not move
They were there for one another
They seemed like a couple
They move together in the same direction
The mystery pair
We carried on walking
They started to walk as well
The next day
We bumped into the mystery pair again
They were in the same spot
They seemed to be a couple
I called them Mr and Mrs the day before
I called them the Mystery pair today
The two ducks seemed to have made a home
They dominated that area
They seemed to have made it home
And if I came back the next day
I am sure they will still be there
The other ducks move around from
Place to place
But the mystery pair remain
The mystery pair

Composed in my Villa in France on 23/04/19
Inspired to write following my morning walk

Beauty within Alien 175

Alien object timed
Hard exterior
Heart gold
Layers transform humans
Glitter lit up the room
Marble indicate freshness
Green indicate life
Grey define character
Glitter beauty within
Formed layers
Friendships supportive
Object not an Alien
Transforms life
Through many layers
Colours
Tough exterior
Fine interior
Beauty within Alien

*Composed in the Bring Home poetry group
workshop on 27/04/2019
Composed from concrete poetry from a stone*

Our Anniversary 176

27 years has gone by just like that
It's been an amazing time
With my lifelong friend, husband, father, partner to our family
The father of my three children
I thank God for our union
He chose him and he has not been a disappointment
He is a blessing
I adore him as a partner
I love him from my heart
He has made my life beautiful
He is an ever-present help
He is always by my side
He has been there on all occasions that are important to me
Birthdays, vacations, anniversaries, weddings, charity walks,
party's poetry
Funerals what can I say
He is the one that God made for me
I pray we have many more years of happiness and joy
together
God bless our union
God bless our marriage
Thank God for all you have done for us
Happy Anniversary to us

**Composed on the train on 02/05/19 on the eve of
our 27th Wedding Anniversary**

My First Poetry Anniversary 177

It's exactly a year ago I went to Gidea Park
I started to write from a park bench
I am not what I was once I am not where I need to be
But God is in the Gap he is leading the way
I joined the Poetry Alchemy Online group this year with over 230 poets worldwide
I was invited to join the Foxes poetry group this year
I joined the Creative writing group this year in my local area
I self-published my first poetry book
I am described by some as a world traveller
I am well received in the international circuit
I have been around promoting my poetry to different groups Poetic insight, Growing Poetry, spoken word London, Poetry Home group to mention a few
I have a book page which has been very supportive on this journey
I have learnt different styles of poems
Split poems, Condensed poems, object poetry, work poetry, Smell Poetry and created around 177 poems to date
I have met some amazing people on my journey who have also contributed to my poems through their acknowledgements and reviews on my book
I have also produced a huge online platform attracting 1 million members which was quite instrumental
My poems featured on the following platforms
The talent bank, creative writing and ...
I have a You tube channel where I promote my poems
My book has travelled around a lot and the feedback has been great
I have entered several competitions
I have also big online book promotion this year reaching a huge audience of over 12500.
I have helped my local community to promote their businesses through my book launch this year
I am grateful to God and everyone who has liked or listened to my poems in the first year Happy first Poetry Anniversary to me #JourneysofLife
Has taken people on a journey and has been compared to other poets
It's is inspirational motivational and transformational

Composed at home on 4th May 2019 on the eve
of my first poetry writing anniversary

The Beauty in the Lake 178

She swam towards us
In elegance and whiteness
The ducks gave way to her
The bread in the water
She glides across the stream
The birds are peeking in the woods
The noise from nature filled the air
The green of colours
The brown grass overshadows the lake
The beauty was beholding as she arrives
The neck submerged
The beak is pink and rounded
She glides amongst the ducks
The Swan is a beauty in a class of its own
We waited for her arrival
As she saw us, she came towards us
The birds were named Peter and Paul
The Swan the beauty on the lake
We saw her before and wanted to catch up
with her again
The beauty on the lake
Watch out for the beauty of nature that
surrounds you

Composed on the train on 07/05/19
Inspired to write following our walk-in nature

The Rastafarian Dude on the Flight to Malaga 179

We arrived at our seats on the flight to Malaga
We were welcomed with a smile
Our seats 22E and 22F
He got up and we settled
Our seat belts on
He was a character
Dressed in Jamaican colours
In white skin with a Rasta as long to his back
Headphones in
Playing music on his phone
Nodding away as we flew
Seat belts sign off
Buckles off and off he went to the bathroom from 22D
Panicky and nervous he seemed
Head in his palm for most of the flight
Smiles a lot which was good to see
Sweets he had on his flight to Malaga
Struck me as a musician or DJ
But too scared to ask
The Rastafarian dude on the flight to Malaga

Composed on the flight to Malaga 14/05/2019
Inspired to write from noting my flight passenger

The Sports Cars on the Drive 180
Fast and Furious

The hotel was inviting
As we dropped off our cases
We were met with different cars
Porsche
Lamborghini
Bumble bees
Mercedes Benz
All parked along the drive leading into the reception
Was curious to know what was going on?
The cars apparently belonged to guests
I thought there was a car show
Or the rides were for hire
They came in different colours
I took a picture with the white Porsche
The cars were beautiful, fast and furious
I would have loved to test drive one of them to
Marbella or Puerto Banus
What a lovely sight to see
A group of fast cars on your drive on vacation
Never seen anything like it before
The sports cars on the drive
I was gutted I hadn't taken many photos
As I don't think I will ever see or have the opportunity
to see them again
I will make sure not to lose such an opportunity again

*Inspired to write following sighting of a group of fast
and furious cars on the drive in Marbella 15/05/19*

My Flowers came with me to Marbella 181

I left my flowers at home on my dining table
I took a picture as they had blossomed just before we left
They looked four times the size I had received them on my hubbys birthday
They gave off a lovely floral smell as you walked into the room
I did not want to part with them to be honest
But I had to as I was leaving for Marbella
I called my older son to water them daily and send me a photo
As we arrived at the hotel
I observed the floral smell in the room
As I approached, I noticed the big flowers in reception
I observed they were exactly the same flowers I had left at home on my centre piece
God always has a plan
He knew I had not finished with those flowers
He planted one for me on arrival at Marbella
I would go to reception to look at my flowers daily
It would seem God always has a plan for you and me
I am grateful that I still have my flowers at Marbella
My flowers followed me to Marbella
My flowers were waiting for me in Marbella
God had a purpose in this
What can you remember that is so fulfilling, that gives you joy?
My flowers came with me to Marbella

Inspired to write seeing my flowers in Marbella
Composed in my hotel room in Marbella

Senegalese Boys on Levante Beach 182

We came out from el Cortes ingles
We bumped into the boys
Selling bags, wallets, side bags and other
leather goods
The boys worked very close together
I wanted and ordered a back pack
He called his friend to bring me the brown bag I
wanted
We carried on our journey
We arrived at the harbour
We bumped into two Senegalese boys
We stopped to price the bags
I carried on to the fish restaurant
As we sat at the fish restaurant the Senegalese
They brought belts, back bags, different
handbags and all sorts
What we noticed was how the boys call each
other and exchange bags
It was like they worked as a team
As one of the boys, moved another one arrives
It was like they were there for each other
They supported each other, and wanted to make
a sale for each other
The boys were like a small community
They had made it home in Puerto Banus
I will encourage you to patronise them on your
visit to Levante beach if you can
The Senegalese community in Puerto Banus

Composed in my hotel on 16/05/2019
Inspired to write following my experience on
Levante beach

The Party 183

The party in Marbella
We flew to a beautiful location
It was an amazing view from our balcony
We could watch the sea flow in all directions
We saw the boats
We met the other guests
We had a meet and greet
There were events planned for everyone
We had a party bag on arrival
There was food and drink for everyone
We went for golf in the morning
There was a golf tournament for the professionals
Some played Tennis
Some went sight seeing
There was something for everyone
The party time closed in
We met and were served Canapés
There was fish, samosa, ham, nuts, prawns
There was a pool in the background
They served, served and served
The service was fantastic
There was time for photos
There was time to network and socialise
It was a beautiful day for a lovely party
We had a fantastic time
There was beautiful music for everyone
We danced, danced and danced
The celebrant was relaxed and made us all feel welcome
It was an opportunity to take a short break
We went to the port of Puerto Banus
We spent a day in the spa
There was so much thought that had gone into the planning
of this event
It was the Party to be
We were there
The Party in Marbella

Composed in my hotel room in Marbella on 18/05/19
Inspired to write following the party

Two Birds at the Breakfast Bar 184

We went for breakfast on our first morning in Marbella 184
There were two brown Robins that came for breakfast too
They would fly on the Chandelier
They would pick food crumbs off the floor
They would sit on the table
They would fly across the room
The vacationers made them feel welcome
The vacationers never frowned at them
But rather would let them be
They flew out of the room on to the sea
The next day we sat at the bar for lunch with friends
The two birds were there again sitting on the chair
I named them Peter and Paul
They sat and watched
There were olives left on one of the tables
There were olives on the floor
One of the birds picked up an olive from the floor with his beak and flew away with it
Then Paul picked up some cheese and flew away towards the beach
These two birds behaved as humans
They were not afraid of us
Nor were we afraid of them
We co exist together
There is enough room in the world for everyone
When we give each other space to grow?
The two Robins at the breakfast bar
They had become friends with the guests
They had become neighbours with the staff
They were company for the golfers
They made life easy as they did not interfere
The Robins at the breakfast bar reminded me of the rhyme
There were two black birds

Composed on the flight back to Stanstead on 19/05/19
Inspired to write following sighting of the two birds at the breakfast bar

The Tunnels 185

We drove onto Guadalmina from the airport
We approached a Tunnel on our 45-minute drive
The next day we took a drive to Puerto Banus harbour
We missed our way and had to drive 10km
We approached another tunnel called Santa Maria
The Tunnels over here were extra long
They were white dark and well-lit at the same time
They went on for a long time that you could feel the
sense of the darkness within them
As we approached the end of the tunnel you could feel
the ray of light as it shone through the dark
You could feel the sense of the saying
There is light at the end of the tunnel
It made me think I was going to compose this on
vacation but then I didn't
I did not want to drop it as it made sense to compose it
So many can be going through a tunnel but there is
always a way out
No matter how long it takes to get there
There is always light at the end of the tunnel
Without light there cannot be darkness
I want to assure you to hang in there and drive through
that journey
The tunnels
There were loads of tunnels in Marbella and we drove
through them all
Are you going through a tunnel?
can you see the light at the end of the tunnel?

Inspired to write following my vacation in Marbella
Composed at the bus stop in Collier row

Smell was my Prompt 186

Blackfriars bridge
Lovely day
Boats under the bridge
Tourists around
Music playing
Colours blooming
Dance moves and steps
Families and children
Culture in the making
Diversity of Nations
People having fun
Photographers everywhere
Sky is blue
Clouds amazing
Aeroplane on the move
Crowd having fun
Tried a plate of Paella
Prawns and Mussels not my favourite
Queues everywhere
Churros Coffee
Try new things
Nice atmosphere
Had a coffee
Took some photos
Nice day out
Blackfriars bridge
Amazing views
Spanish Festival

*Inspired to write following a day out with my
poetry group on 25/05/19
Composed in the Fish house restaurant*

The Two Ladies Communication 187

As I sat on the train
On my way to work
On my phone
I noticed two ladies
Sitting next to me
I noticed they were speaking
But not talking
I noticed they were communicating
In their own way
Their own style
I noticed they were smiling
But not laughing
In their own way
They were having a conversation
It took me a while to understand what was going on
They were conversing using sign language
Sometimes in my culture
You don't have to talk to be understood
You don't have to speak for your child to understand you
You could use your eyes and a child would understand
You could be friends and you understand each other
You can be in a relationship and you understand one another
You hear when people say we connect with each other in
The two Ladies in the train were deaf or hard of hearing passengers having a normal conversation
95% of all communication is body language

Composed on the platform on 31/05/19
Having witnessed two deaf ladies on the train the day before

The Blue Motorised Tricycle 188

I had seen it before on a Sunday at the traffic light few
months ago
I forgot about it
I took a photo
Few months down the line
I come across the same blue motor bike
And then I took a photo
And then few weeks later
I decide to compose a poem
It's interesting how you see things in life and do nothing
about them
The thought stays with you in your memory
And then few months down the line
The thought comes up again
And then you wonder why you hadn't done anything
about that good idea you had
Sometimes God is putting an idea or thought in our
minds and wants to see our reaction
It's like the parable of the sower in the bible
Where God gives you an investment or talent and wants
to see what you do with the idea
So, when you have an idea
Run with your idea just like the man on his Blue
motorcycle
I hope I bump into him the third time and see what
happens next
Have you a thought or idea you have been holding on to
Have you an idea that's been manifesting
It's time to take that move as the green light is there and
that's when the bike moves
Keep moving
The blue motorbike
I decided to compose on the bus today

*Inspire to write following sighting the bike the second
time at the same light*

Pebbles 189

Walking past this morning
The bridge overlooking the clouds
The men walk past the bridge
The sun appears under the cloud
We walk past the man and his dog
We arrive at the house with pebbles
The pebbles on the drive
Remind me of gravels on the drive
The crunch noise they make
The different size of stones
The different colours of white, brown and grey
The tree amid the pebbles
The neighbours wonder why
The shoes on the drive
The pebbles make such a difference to the house
The house stands out
The pebbles make the house stand out
I wonder what makes you stand out from the crowd
I wonder what makes a difference in your life?
What are you thankful for?
The pebbles on the drive
The pebbles stand out from the rest
The pebbles

I was inspired to write this poem
following our walk on 08/06/2019

The Cat on the Drive 190

She catches my attention
As I walk past the house with the black door
The house on the corner
Never observed the cat on the drive
Her fur as white as snow
She had a peculiar look
Black and white head
Her eyes were striking yellow
Brown feet
She stood out as we walked past
She did not move
She kept her gaze on me
I went back to take her photo
She was still there
I thought I would write a poem about the cat
The Cat on the drive
Have you a pet
Do you have pets living with you?
What is so special about your pet?
They make great company to any one
The Cat on the drive

Inspired to write following our walk
Composed at Costco on 07/06/2019

The Electric Bikes in London 191

It was our staff event
As we walked back to Monument
There were workers having fun
It was a Friday
There were bikes parked for hire
I noticed they were different
I took a photo
As it reminded me of the environment
It reminded me of electric cars
And as such our environment needs to be safer
For the future generations
Our environments have been taken over by
pollution
You must pay a congestion charge if you travel at
certain times into central London
You also must pay a higher amount on your car if
the engine causes pollution
It was such a good idea to see an electric bike in
central London on my journey
From the staff event
The electric bikes in London
Were painted in neon

Composed on the park bench on 22/06/19
Inspired to write following our staff event

Our New Road 192

It was such a nice evening
On my evening walk
We approached our new road
It was just tarmacked
The white lines have just been marked on white
I stood in the middle of the road
I looked up and I looked down
The road was like a valley
I did not feel
Threatened by traffic
It was nice to stand and take in the view
I took a picture of my journey
Sometimes we need to be at risk
In order to move sometimes
We need to challenge ourselves
Sometimes you need to take the deep end and feel
vulnerable
Ideas would come afterwards
It would push you in the right direction
If a car were to arrive you would have to move
It becomes uncomfortable then you would act
Our new road

Composed in the park on 21/06/19
Inspired to write following our new road

Town Centre 193

Stratford
I have worked here on and off
I have seen the changes
The new buildings
The new roads
The cycle lanes
The new buses
The place has completely been transformed
From what I used to know
And what it is now
I love Stratford
It connects you to many places
It's quite close to central London
It's easy to get to
I did most of my videos here.
On the train, on the platform, on the cycle lane
It's been transformed
There are open spaces for all
I sat and had a break one morning
And noticed the benches
Noticed how the roundabout was different
There were plants that made such a huge difference
The homeless crowd seemed to have reduced in that
location
I wonder if it became too pretty
Or too open
Or they just moved on
The town centre has been transformed
It makes such a huge difference
What have you noticed on your way out today?
That makes a difference to you
Or makes a difference to your community
The Town centre

Composed at home 02/07/19

Beautiful Sunset 194

We went to the wedding
It was a beautiful day
It was a beautiful venue
The three Rivers golf and country club
We had a fantastic time
Canapés, food and drink
Nice people and a good atmosphere
We drove home through the plush green
We arrived on the A127
As we approached, I saw this beautiful circle
above the road
It looked amazing
As we got closer, the sun got smaller
The sky was blue
The clouds were set
It was such an amazing view
I called it the beautiful sunset
I took a photo and decided to write a poem the
next day
The Beautiful sunset on our way home from the
wedding
What amazes you in the day
As you journey through
Do you stop and enjoy the moments?
Or do you just walk through them?

Composed in my living room
Inspired to write following my walk on 06/07/19

The Flower Girls 195

It was a beautiful day
At the wedding
The venue was beautiful
The bridge on the fountain
The Roses graced the day
The Roses were everywhere
The cake was white as snow
The bridesmaid in lilac
The flower girls
Two of them
With their baskets
In their champagne coloured dresses
Came with confetti
Sprinkled on the floor
They looked adorable
They were playful
They were fearless
They brought child fullness to the occasion
They were flawless
They were innocent
They were happy
They were carefree
They had no problems
They were just effortless
And made my day
Wherever I saw them
They were happy and contented
The flower girls

Composed at the wedding
Inspired to write at home on 06/07/19

Couples 196

I was walking down the street
I observed three generations
Three couples holding hands
Reminds me of
The three musketeers
Three wisemen
Charlie's Angels
Threesomes
All the trios
It was interesting to see three couples together
It was too late to take a picture
As it was such an unusual sight
I pondered on it for days
I discussed it with my son one morning on the
train
So, I decided to compose a poem
The three couples in love holding hands along
the high road
Were they three generations?
Were they parents and children?
Or were they just on vacation
The three couples amazed me
It's good to do things in unison

Composed on the train on 20/06/19
Inspired to write following an experience

The Christmas Trees in the Car park 197

The Car Park
The Gym
The Blood Van
My sons park their car on their way to work
On my way to the city
We have always parked here
For years as a family
We all drive
Except my daughter
But we have never noticed the trees
The trees act as a fence
The trees act as a barrier
The trees are close to the sky
The trees are in a row
On this morning as we walked to the station
I noticed the trees in the car park
They look like Christmas' trees
They were reminders it was six months to
Christmas
We were in July
The Christmas trees in the car park
The Christmas trees that act as a barrier
The Christmas trees beautify the skyline
When you park your car
Check out the car park area

Composed at home
Inspired to write following sighting of the trees

The Amputee with a Stride 198

It was at Fairlop station
I was on the platform
She came off the train
In camouflage shorts
She seemed to be an ex veteran
I was walkinag behind her
As we approached the stairs
I noticed she had lost a limb
She embraced her features
I saw her sitting later by the gym
I thought she was having a break
Or she was having a fag
She smiled as I walked past
The Amputee with a stride
Had embraced her disability

Composed on the train on 11/07/19
Inspired to write following sighting

Centre Court #our experience 199

My love for tennis
Our passions brought us together
We had been three years ago
We sat on Henman Hill
We enjoyed our time the last time
But this year was different
There had been changes and development
The champions chair was new
The photo booth with trophies was new
The Pride flag was new
The team water strawberries all made the
experience worthwhile
We had a blast on our second visit
We were invited to sit in Centre court by the
stewards
It was a dream come true
We took our seats on centre stage
We were on the best court in history
We were amazed that we had been wishing to do
this for years
And then we were invited
We enjoyed the doubles match on Centre court
We took photos from our seats
We did a video to remind us of our visit to the best
court in history
Wimbledon 2019
Centre court #ourexperience
What has your experience of Centre court been ?
What experience have you had in your lifetime
that has surprised you?

*Inspired to write following my second visit to
Wimbledon*
Composed on the bus on 14/07/19

Pride in Wimbledon 200

Pride was celebrated across the globe
Toronto New York
50 years of Pride celebration in London
The colours are radiant
Celebrating diversity
Celebration LGBT
The pride flags demonstrate acceptance
The pride colours are unique to Pride
I had my pride hat on at the staff event
I noticed the pride colours at Mile End station
on my way to work
You are free to love who you want to love
And you are free to be who you want to be
Pride is an opportunity to celebrate our diversity
as humans
It's a means to celebrate love
And to see the Pride flag in Wimbledon was a
bonus
That such a huge event that attracts people
worldwide is in acceptance of Pride

It caught my attention
So, I thought to write a poem about
The Pride flag in Wimbledon

Composed at home on 14/07/19
Inspired to write following my visit to
Wimbledon

Printed in Poland
by Amazon Fulfillment
Poland Sp. z o.o., Wrocław